Those Footnotes in Your New Testament

A Textual Criticism Primer for Everyone

Thomas W. Hudgins

In Memory of
Howard Barefoot

Energion Publications
Gonzalez, Florida
2017

ISBN10:1-63199-374-7
ISBN13: 978-1-63199-374-9

Energion Publications
P. O. Box 841
Gonzalez, FL 32560

energion.com
pubs@energion.com

TABLE OF CONTENTS

1

INTRODUCTION

What do those occasional footnotes in your New Testament talking about "texts" and "manuscripts" mean? Why are they even there? When I flip to Mark 16 in my New American Standard Bible, I have a note at the bottom of the page that says this: "A few late mss and versions contain this paragraph, usually after v. 8; a few have it at the end of ch." What does that mean? We find similar notes in places like Matthew 5:22, John 7:53–8:11, and even the last verse in Revelation. The Revised Standard Version has notes like "Other/some ancient manuscripts add/omit . . . ." My New King James Bible uses notes like "NU-Text omits 'You shall not bear false witness'" in Romans 13:9.

Maybe you never noticed those little notes, or perhaps just paid them very little attention. It is possible though that you had an experience similar to the one I had shortly after God saved me. I was at a Bible study with a bunch of other college students, and each of us was taking turns reading aloud from our New Testaments. I remember one of my friends had just finished reading, and someone else spoke up: "Hey, that's not what mine says." One of them was reading from the New American Standard, and the other one was reading from the New King James. We realized that we were not looking at a translation issue. This was different. There were actual words present in one that were not present in the other.

For this reason we have something called textual criticism. The purpose of this book is threefold. First, we want to look at why we have these notes in the first place. If the Bible is inspired (2 Timothy 3:16), why do we have notes talking about some saying one thing and others saying something else? We will look at the need for textual criticism. Second, we want to talk about what textual criticism is and the criteria that we use for evaluating different textual issues as we encounter them in the New Testament. And third, we want to engage some of the misconceptions dealing with textual criticism, especially the claim that the Bible has errors. Textual criticism is important—not just for pastors and teachers, but for every single student of God's Word. Not everyone needs to be an expert in this area of exegesis, but we should all have an understanding of what textual criticism is, why it is important, and how we know that we can trust our Bibles!

2
Explaining the Need for Textual Criticism

I recently flipped through the Gospel of Matthew in my copy of the Holman Christian Standard Bible just to see how many textual notes were found in the footnotes. In that Gospel alone there are a total of 115, one in every single chapter except for Chapter 7.[1] Needless to say, this is not an uncommon occurrence. In Matthew 1, for example, we can see a few types of different readings. In Matthew 1:6 there is a question about whether Matthew refers to David with the title "king" or without it. In Matthew 1:7–10, there is a question about the name of two individuals: (1) a descendant of Abijah—spelled Asa or Asaph—in 1:7–8; and (2) a descendant of Manasseh—spelled Amon or Amos—in 1:10. And when we drop down to Matthew 1:25, there is a question as to whether Matthew refers to Jesus simply as Mary's "son" or her "firstborn son." Now these are not representative of all of the types of textual issues found in Matthew or the rest of the New Testament. We will focus on others as we continue our study. But we can make two observations based on these examples. First, there are questions about what the authors of the New Testament texts wrote in *certain* places, not every word or verse. We have to ask the question, "Why does this issue exist, especially if the Bible is inspired by God?" Before we answer that question, though, here is the second observation: The trustworthiness of the New Testament is not at stake with issues like the ones found in Matthew 1. An examination of the whole

---

1 Matt. 1:6, 7, 8, 10, 25; 2:18; 3:16; 4:10; 5:22, 25, 44 [2 total], 47; 6:1, 4, 6, 13, 15, 18, 33; 8:18, 23, 28, 29; 9:8, 13, 35; 10:3; 11:15, 19; 12:4, 15, 31, 35, 47; 13:9, 43, 51, 55; 14:12, 22, 24, 30; 15:4, 6 [2 total], 8, 14, 16, 22, 39; 16:2–3 [2 total], 4, 13, 20; 17:4, 8, 9, 11 [2 total], 20, 21, 22, 26; 18:11, 15, 29, 35; 19:4, 9, 17 [2 total], 20, 29; 20:6, 7, 16, 19, 22, 23; 21:12, 44; 22:7, 13, 30, 32, 44; 23:4, 5, 8, 14, 19, 26 [2 total]; 24:36, 42; 25:13, 31; 26:3, 28, 42 [2 total], 60 [2 total]; 27:2, 16, 17, 24, 34, 35, 41, 42, 58; 28:9.

New Testament would yield the same conclusion. Simply stated, we can trust our Bibles.

The two most important passages in the New Testament dealing with biblical inspiration are 2 Timothy 3:16 and 2 Peter 1:20–21:

> "All Scripture is inspired by God and profitable for teaching, reproof, correction, and training in righteousness." (2 Timothy 3:16)

> "But know this first of all: No prophecy of Scripture is a matter of one's own interpretation, for no prophecy was ever made by an act of human will alone, but men moved by the Holy Spirit spoke from God." (2 Peter 1:20–21)

When we talk about "inspiration," we are talking about God's role in the composition of the books of the Bible. Paul tells us that everything that is written down in them has as their ultimate author none other than God himself. Sure, when Matthew wrote his Gospel, the reed pen was in his hands. But there was an unseen author who guided Matthew in what he wrote. That is why Peter talks about "prophecy of Scripture" in his letter. The biblical texts come to us like prophecies came to people in the early church— God revealed a specific message to a single individual who in turn communicated that message to group of individuals for whom the message was intended. The only difference between biblical inspiration and prophecy is the former is written down to preserve that message through time and for all Christian communities. Peter lets us know that Matthew did not write the Gospel of Matthew on his own. The message being recorded was ultimately God's; it was just channeled through a chosen human instrument. Matthew, just like every other author of a biblical text, was like a reed in the hand of God.

So God played a huge role in the writing of the New Testament. And so did Matthew, Luke, Mark, John, Paul, Peter, James, and Jude. Scripture would not be Scripture without their joint roles. When we say that the Bible is "inspired," we are talking about the original texts that were written.[2] That is an important point. We are not talking about the copies that were made of those originals. Today all we have are copies. No original manuscript[3] is known to exist today. And this explains why we have all of these notes in our Bibles today in the twenty-first century: As these copies were made, different readings slipped into the texts. Sometimes changes to a text were accidental, sometimes they were intentional. We need to remember that anytime something is copied, there is a risk of the copy not being exactly like the original.

When we think about how often the New Testament manuscripts were copied for preservation and distribution, we should not be surprised that there are certain questions about the original wording in certain places. J. K. Elliott writes the following:

> As is the case with all ancient literatures, the biblical works have not survived in one immutable, original, inviolate form. Textual critics have to work back from the manuscripts, translations and quotations of those books which we possess.[4]

Notice Elliott points out that this issue surrounding the original wording of the New Testament texts is not something unique to the New Testament. It is not some strange phenomenon. On the contrary, every ancient text has this issue.

Before the invention of the printing press in the fifteenth century, all writing was reproduced and preserved exclusively by hand. In other words, no MacBooks and no Xerox. León Vaganay and

---

2 There is an interesting article by Michael A. Grisanti regarding inspiration and editorial activity vs. scribal activity with respect to the Old Testament texts. The traditional view of the divine inspiration of a discourse (an author sitting down to write the discourse, the final result being that which was written by his hand without any editorial changes by second hands) better explains what took place with the New Testament texts. The inspiration of Old Testament texts is a little more complicated, but Grisanti's study is very clear at explaining these unique dynamics. See Michael A. Grisanti, "Inspiration, Inerrancy, and the OT Canon: The Place of Textual Updating in an Inerrant View of Scripture," *JETS* 44:4 (Dec 2001): 577–598.
3 Original manuscripts are also referred to as *autographs*.
4 J. K. Elliott, *New Testament Textual Criticism: The Application of Thoroughgoing Principles*, Supplement to *Novum Testamentum* 137, ed. M. M. Mitchell and D. P. Moessner (Leiden: Brill, 2010), 13.

Christian-B. Amphoux help us put the New Testament in perspective with a comparison to other ancient texts:

> In point of fact, the lapse of time between the original documents and the copies which have been handed down is relatively short: at worst, 250 years or so, since whole manuscripts from the fourth century have survived; and at best, no more than 100 years in the case of papyri dating from around AD 200. In this respect, no other work of early classical literature is in such a favourable position. There is a gap of over 1,000 years between the original composition and the extant manuscripts of the writings of Euripides, Sophocles, Aeschylus, Aristophanes, Thucydides, Plato and Demosthenes. With the Latin authors, the picture is slightly less bleak, but still not nearly as good as the situation of the New Testament writings. The gap is well over three centuries for the writings of Virgil, which are the best preserved.[5]

No original manuscripts exist. That is true. But the transmission of the New Testament texts is a feat unparalleled in world history. No one throws out the value of Euripides or Plato in Western philosophy simply because there are questions about the original wording of their texts in certain places. The situation of the New Testament is quite remarkable. No originals exist, but we have copies of those manuscripts that were written not long after the original composition. In fact, no other ancient text has so short a time period between original composition and extant copy. The issue in textual criticism surrounds the changes that took place during transmission. And all ancient literature experienced changes from original composition to subsequent copies. Consider the words of Francesco Robortello (1516–1567): "[I]f books written by the hand of ancient authors existed, we would labor less."[6] Indeed, if originals of the texts of the New Testament existed today, textual

---

5   León Vaganay and Christian-B. Amphoux, *An Introduction to New Testament Textual Criticism*, trans. Jenny Heimerdinger (New York: Cambridge University Press, 1991), 2.

6   Francesco Robortello, *De arte sive tatione corrigenda antiquorum libros disputatio*, ed. G. Pompella (Naples: Luigi Loffredo Editore, 1975), 44, cited by Tim William Machan, *Textual Criticism and Middle English Texts* (Charlottesville, VA: University Press of Virginia, 1994), 20.

criticism would be of no consequence to the study and exegesis of the New Testament. Unfortunately, there are no originals. And so it is extremely important to our study of the New Testament.

Copying the texts of the New Testament began immediately after they were written. The first Gospel that was written was the Gospel of Matthew. It was designed as a discipleship resource to be used among the communities in which the gospel was proclaimed and embraced. Jesus' words at the end of the Gospel serve as the purpose of the Gospel—"As you go [into the world] train all the nations, baptizing them in the name of the Father, the Son, and the Holy Spirit, *teaching them to put into practice everything I commanded you*" (Matthew 28:19–20a). This served as the first training resource of the early church. As they went out from Judea, they would carry the Gospel of Matthew with them to the places in the world where Jesus sent them. And when they left those communities, copies of it were left so the people in those communities could study for themselves and teach about the Master.

There are other examples in the New Testament of these texts being copied. Paul appears to quote Luke (though probably Matthew) in 1 Timothy 5:18: "The laborer is worthy of his wages" (cf. Leviticus 19:13; Deuteronomy 24:15; Matthew 10:10; Luke 10:7).[7] If he is quoting a Gospel, then Paul must have had a copy of his own. Peter is also familiar with the letters of Paul, having viewed them when he saw Peter in Jerusalem or Rome or having

---

7   He also references this teaching in 1 Cor. 9:14. In other places where Paul quotes the teaching of Jesus, he refers to it as the "message of the Lord" (1 Thess. 4:15) or specifies that it was delivered directly to him from the Lord (1 Cor. 11:23–25). In 1 Tim. 5:18, however, he specifically refers to this teaching as "Scripture" (γραφή), which refers to the message of God in written form.

It is possible that the quote is from Matthew. Let me briefly explain how: Matthew uses the Greek word for "food" or "nourishment" (τροφή *trophē*), but Luke has the word (μισθός *misthos*) that people in the first century naturally associated with remuneration in general. Paul could be quoting Matthew, but he decided to use the word "wages" instead, capturing the idea of what Jesus meant by his agricultural proverb. Paul just clarifies it for the Greek-speaking world: Jesus was not just talking about food. He was talking about remuneration in general. And that would explain why Luke had earlier used the word he did when he wrote the Gospel—Paul, his mentor, had been using it when he taught.

come into contact with them as he traveled to various places (2 Peter 3:15–16). Paul also instructed churches to share letters: "And once this letter has been read among you, see that it is read in the church of the Laodiceans; and you read the letter from Laodicea too" (Colossians 4:16). Someone would have copied it and exchanged it for a copy of the one written to the other church. And Paul probably maintained a copy of every letter he wrote.[8] In other words, he did not just write a letter and send it off. He understood that what he wrote came from God and was profitable for every Christian community and every individual believer. When he visited a locality, someone in the community was able to copy those letters and keep them for study and instruction. The first churches to copy Revelation are those found in Revelation 2–3. The order in which the churches appear follows the travel route one would make if they left Patmos, landed in Ephesus, and then worked their way to Laodicea. The whole of Revelation would be copied as each messenger carried it from one city to the next (and everyone who heard it was warned against adding or taking away from the words of the book [Revelation 22:18–19]). Every single one of the New Testament texts was written for instruction.

Copying the texts of the New Testament continued for over fifteen hundred years—all over the world, wherever the gospel had spread. And each time a manuscript was copied presented an opportunity for transcriptional mistakes and intentional changes to its contents. In fact, it is more likely than not that this occurred to some extent each time a manuscript was copied. Textual criticism is necessary because we do not have the original manuscripts of the New Testament texts. We have copies—the great and the great, great, and the great, great, great (etc.) grandchildren of the originals—and those copies contain numerous different readings. Since the New Testament is inspired by God and foundational for the Christian life, it behooves us to do everything we can to figure out the original state of those texts.

---

8   In fact, one option for Paul's reference to the "parchments" (μεμβράνας *membranas*) in 2 Tim. 4:13 is they refer to his personal letters. That Paul (or one of his closest associates) maintained a copy of his letters does not hinge on this interpretation though.

Before we turn our attention to the criteria for analyzing a textual issue, it is important to highlight some of the more significant textual issues of the New Testament. After all, if they were all just issues of spelling or word order, then textual analysis would not be quite as important as it is. It would be more a noble pursuit than anything else. The following are just a sample of some more significant (though not necessarily the most important) textual issues.

1. *A letter issue.* Sometimes a single letter can make all the difference. An example of this is found in John 1:41 with the word "first." Without going into all of the intricacies of the Greek language, just remember that the function of words is connected to how they are spelled (in particular, certain endings), not word order like we see in the English language. With that in mind, some manuscripts spell "first" πρῶτος (*prōtos*) and others πρῶτον (*prōton*). Now if the first reading is original, it means the word "first" is modifying the subject of the sentence—"He" (referring to Andrew in v. 40). If the second reading is original, it means "first" is modifying the predicate of the sentence—"found his own brother Simon." So we have two options. (1) Did John say that Andrew was the first of the two disciples who left John the Baptist to follow Jesus who went and got his own brother? In other words, it would imply that the other disciple must have had a brother as well, and that must mean that he is identifying himself as the other disciple (since he too had a brother, John of Zebedee). Or (2) Did John say that the very first thing Andrew did, when invited to come and see where Jesus was staying and spend the day with him, was tell Jesus to hang on a quick moment while he went off to get his brother? If this reading is correct, it seems that Andrew understood that there was something more important than just spending time with Jesus; he wanted others to meet Jesus too. The only thing that could make spending time with Jesus more amazing would be if others could spend time with him too.

2. *A word issue.* Sometimes a word is found in some manuscripts but not in others. And sometimes this can change everything about the way we understand a passage in the New Testament. One such example is found in Matthew 5:22. Almost every translation reads like this: "But I say to you that everyone who is angry with

his brother will be guilty before the court [or subject to judgment etc.]." At first glance it looks as if Jesus is condemning all anger. To get angry must mean that a person has sinned, right? Well, problems arise when we encounter passages like Matthew 21:12–13, where Jesus throws people out of the temple, and Mark 3:5, which indicates that Jesus looked "with anger" at those assembled in a synagogue. If all anger is sinful, then what about Jesus' anger? There lies the issue. But some translations—admittedly very few—have something different. The ISV, for example, reads this way: "But I say to you that everyone who is angry with his brother without a cause will be subject to punishment." Notice the words "without a cause." Those words translate a single Greek word (εἰκῇ *eikē*) that is found in a number of manuscripts. Some manuscripts have εἰκῇ, some do not. And committees for translations that include it, like the ISV, have decided based on the evidence that the word is original to the Gospel of Matthew. Either Jesus condemned all anger or only anger that was not justified. It matters a lot.

3. *A phrase issue.* Sometimes there is a question about whether a whole phrase is original or not. The phrases "in Ephesus" in Ephesians 1:1 and "in Rome" in Romans 1:7 are examples of this. Some manuscripts have them, some do not. Both of these phrases occur in the prescript section of the letters, which identifies the author and audience. Take "in Ephesus" for example. If the phrase is not original to the letter, then it changes the way we study the letter.[9] Do any of the socio-cultural practices that were characteristic of Ephesus in the first century have any bearing on one's understanding of passages such as Ephesians 5:18–21, where Paul exhorts believers to stop getting drunk with wine and instead let their lives be influenced by the Holy Spirit? If the phrase is original, then the answer is yes. If not, then background information regarding the city of Ephesus would not help anyone better understand the meaning of this passage.

And there are issues surrounding clauses (e.g., "who spent all her living on physicians" in Luke 8:43), whole verses (e.g., whether or not Luke 23:34 is original or not), whole paragraphs (e.g., John

---

9   For a discussion on the steps of exegesis, see Thomas W. Hudgins' "The Ten Exegetical Steps" available at http://www.thomashudgins.com/p/resources.html.

7:53–8:11). There are issues surrounding word order ("No one knows who the Son is except the Father, and who the Father is except the Son" vs. "No one knows who the Father is except the Son, and who the Son is except the Father" in Luke 10:22), the tense of a verb in a given passage (e.g., ". . . among you *stands* [στήκει *stēkei*] one who you do not know" vs. " . . . among you *has stood* [ἕστηκεν *hestēken*] one who you do not know" in John 1:26), and numerous other types of issues related to grammar.

Three textual issues come up again and again in New Testament textual criticism. Their importance is due in part to the size of the discourses in question, but also because of the theological issues related to their content. The first of these, also the shortest, is 1 John 5:7–8, also known as the "Johannine Clause" (Lat. *Comma Johanneum*). John 7:53–8:11 is the second, also known as the "Pericope of the Adulteress" (Lat. *Pericope Adulterae*). And the third is Mark 16:9–20, simply known as "the longer ending of Mark." Each of these are very complex and require more space than this little book affords.[10] Their significance is impossible to miss. For example, if the longer reading of 1 John 5:7–8 which is found in the KJV and NKJV) is original, then that is the most straightforward attestation of the Trinity in all of Scripture.

There is no question that certain textual issues do impact our interpretation of the text. For this reason, textual criticism is a necessary field in New Testament studies. So how do individuals go about studying these issues and based on what evidence do they determine whether a reading is original or not? That is the subject of the next chapter.

---

10 For those interested in reading more about these three textual issues, commentaries on the respective books of the New Testament are a good place to start. See also David Alan Black (ed.), *Perspectives on the Ending of Mark: 4 Views* (Nashville: B&H Academic, 2008); David Alan Black and Jacob N. Cerone (eds.), *The Pericope of the Adulteress in Contemporary Research*, Library of New Testament Studies (New York: Bloomsbury T&T Clark, 2016).

3

EXPLORING THE CRITERIA OF
TEXTUAL CRITICISM

Researchers use what is called "external" and "internal" evidence for evaluating whether or not a reading is original. External evidence deals with the extant manuscript themselves, such as when they were copied, while internal evidence deals with matters like the style and theology of an author. There are seven questions used in weighing the data for a textual issue. The first two are external-evidence questions, the remaining five are internal-evidence questions:

1. Which reading is found in the oldest manuscripts?
2. Which reading is attested to by wider geographical distribution and/or the greatest number of text-types?
3. Which reading is the shortest reading?
4. Which reading is the more difficult reading?
5. Which reading best fits the authors' style and vocabulary?
6. Which reading best fits the author's context and/or theology?
7. Which reading least fits a parallel passage when one is available?

We need to discuss each of these individually in order to get a better grasp of what all is entailed in a textual analysis. But first, how many manuscripts of the New Testament are known to exist today? Actually the precise number is debated, especially since manuscripts are discovered each year, although those discovered are generally later in date. Before the turn of the nineteenth century, scholars knew of only approximately 1,700 Greek manuscripts. The number of Greek manuscripts now exceeds 5,600. To that number we can add thousands of translation manuscripts,[11] lectionary manuscripts, as well as numerous references to New Testament texts by the early church. Most of these manuscripts, we should remember,

---

11 See Bruce M. Metzger's "Index of Versional Manuscripts of the New Testament" in *The Early Versions of the New Testament: Their Origin, Transmission and Limitations* (Oxford: Oxford University Press, 1977), 475–491.

do not contain the entire New Testament corpus—some only have a single book (e.g., the Gospel of Matthew), some more than one book (e.g., just the Gospels or just the letters of Paul), and some only a sliver of a single book (e.g., Luke 4:1–3).

THE CRITERIA

The Date of Manuscripts

Researchers date manuscripts by taking into account a number of different factors: (1) the material on which the text is written; (2) the script; (3) the format of the text on the page; (4) the presence of artwork; etc. The vast majority of extant manuscripts were copied at a later date. Of the more than 5,600 Greek manuscripts listed on the INTF[12] website, more than 5,300 are dated after A.D. 600. Manuscripts that were written on papyrus are generally considered older than vellum or parchment manuscripts, although some papyrus manuscripts were written later than some parchment manuscripts. The majority of the manuscripts that exist today were not written on papyrus. The use of all capital letters is another feature of some of the earliest manuscripts. These manuscripts are known as "majuscules." Oh, and by the way, lots of manuscripts— in an effort to conserve space—did not have any space between the words. Just imagine what it must have been like to read manuscripts with no spaces.

The issue of date is very important to textual criticism. The closer a manuscript is in date to the original composition, the closer it *might be* to the original wording. Just because a manuscript is earlier does not mean that it contains the original reading though. The textual integrity of every manuscript, wherever a textual issue is present, must be subject to a thorough analysis of the evidence regardless of its date, even a very early one. Date is a factor, but it is not the definitive factor.

---

12 The Institut für Neutestamentliche Textforschung (tr. Institute for New Testament Textual Research), located in Westfalia, Germany, is devoted to the study of New Testament manuscripts aimed at determining the original wording of the texts of the New Testament.

Text-Types and the Geographical Distribution of Manuscripts

Researchers group the different manuscripts into categories known as "text-types." Why the categories? Well, they have basically taken the data that is known of the different manuscripts' contents and grouped them together according to their similarities. No category, though, is exactly identical. In fact, there are numerous differences within an individual category. But identifying their unique similarities in a general way helps trace the transmission of the New Testament texts. There are generally three text-types recognized today: (1) Alexandrian, (2) Western, and (3) Byzantine. We can add a fourth text-type called Caesarean, though it is usually limited to the Gospels and some researchers have called into question its existence altogether (and thus its usefulness for thinking through text-critical issues). The vast majority of extant manuscripts belong to the Byzantine text-type. The vast majority of Byzantine manuscripts are later in date, though each text-type—Alexandrian, Western, and Byzantine—contains early witnesses.

As their names indicate, the text-types are generally associated with a particular geographical region too—Alexandrian with Alexandria (Egypt), Western with Rome (Italy) and the churches in that part of the world, Byzantine with the churches of the East, and Caesarean with Caesarea (Israel). And we can assess the readings found in certain early manuscripts and in the writings of early church authors based on their geographical locations, connecting them to the same regions identified for text-types. For example, Origen and Augustine lived in northern Africa, so the readings indicated in their writings would be connected with Alexandria—unless, in the case of Origen, a reading is quoted or alluded to in one of his writings that postdates his move to Caesarea when he was in his forties. But remember, geographical location and text-type are distinct. Wider geographical distribution is more important when considering manuscripts before the end of the fourth century, but wider representation of text-types as a criterion is always important since it is based on the similarities that exist among all manuscripts.

Scholars often discuss the reliability of these different text-types. In fact, many scholars have opted for a preferred text-type because they believe it is more reliable than the others. Since they

14

approach the textual evidence in this way, they immediately lean towards the reading of that text-type. Most researchers today have a proclivity towards the Alexandrian text-type and in particular two manuscripts associated with it, namely Codex Sinaiticus (known by the abbreviations ℵ or 01) and Codex Vaticanus (B or 03).

The Length of a Reading

Which reading is shorter, which is longer? Researchers often ask these questions. Generally speaking, scholars tend to opt for the shorter reading. The argument is that scribes more often added words than omitted them. The question regarding which reading is longer or shorter applies to many of the textual issues in the New Testament. Some issues involve a single letter in a word, which might change how it functions in the sentence or its tense, or an entirely different word being used in one manuscript than another. In either case, the overall length of the reading would remain unchanged. But if there is a question about one word being present in one manuscript but not present in another, then the reading with the word would be considered the longer reading.

There are many reasons why a scribe might intentionally add a word, phrase, clause, and perhaps a whole paragraph. For example, sometimes scribes wanted to (1) reconcile parallel passages in the Gospels; (2) make a text more understandable for their audiences, such as making what they considered an "improvement" to the grammar; (3) add titles to texts that addressed or referred to Jesus (instead of writing "the Lord Jesus" in Revelation 21:21, at least one changed the text to read "our Lord Jesus Christ"); etc. There are also a number of reasons why a scribe might intentionally omit material, and it is important to acknowledge that. For example, if a passage of Scripture did not fit with a particular scribe's theology or view of the Christian life, it is conceivable that they could omit something.

There are no hard and fast rules when it comes to textual criticism. All of the possibilities pertaining to the length of a variant issue must be considered, and this must be done in conjunction with a consideration of all of the evidence—external and internal. For example, almost all of the manuscript evidence supports the inclusion of Matthew 9:34 ("But the Pharisees kept saying, 'He casts out demons by the power of the one who rules the demons'"), but just a smidgen lacks the entire verse. The shorter reading is the one without Matthew 9:34. But the shorter reading is basically limited to a single text-type. How is that explained? A scribe might have thought this statement was redundant, since the Pharisees made the same claim in Matthew 12:44. Maybe that scribe thought it was difficult to explain Jesus' reaction in Matthew 12 (i.e., the unpardonable sin), since he did not react in such a way in Matthew 9. The evidence might suggest that shorter readings, generally speaking, should be preferred over longer readings, but it is just a guiding principle, not a rule. Sometimes the evidence will favor a longer reading, as it does in Matthew 9:34, and that is why those who study these issues need to take all of the evidence into consideration.

The Difficulty of a Reading

When researchers evaluate textual issues, they usually inquire about which reading is more difficult. As a general principle, the more difficult reading should be given serious consideration in light of the other internal and external evidence. When scribes encountered the texts of the New Testament, if they were open to modifying the text, they could have made it more easy or more difficult.

Take Matthew 5:22 for example.[13] Which of the following readings is more difficult?

---

13 For more about this textual issue, see David Alan Black, "Jesus on Anger: The Text of Matthew 5:22a Revisited," *Novum Testamentum* 30 (1988): 1–8; David Alan Black and Thomas W. Hudgins, "Jesus on Anger (Matt 5,22a): A History of Recent Scholarship," in *Greeks, Jews, and Christians: Historical, Religious, and Philological Studies in Honor of Jesús Peláez del Rosal*, ed. L. Roig Lanzillotta and I. Muñoz Gallarte (Córdoba: El Almendro, 2013), 91–104.

| Reading 1: | "But I say to you, anyone who is angry with his brother will be subject to punishment." |
| Reading 2: | "But I say to you, anyone who is angry with his brother <u>without having a justifiable reason</u> will be subject to punishment." |

There are two ways that we can evaluate the difficulty of a reading: (1) based on the transmissional setting and (2) based on the content. Let me explain. Regarding the transmissional setting, we can ask ourselves if it is more difficult to imagine a scribe omitting the word εἰκῇ (*eikē*), which I have translated in Reading 2 as "without having a justifiable reason," or to imagine a scribe adding the word? Well, you could really argue this one either way. It is possible a scribe just overlooked the word as he was copying the text. Just imagine being in a super legalistic community too. Is it not possible that a scribe just wanted Jesus' command to be black and white with no gray in between? It is also possible that a scribe thought about anger as Paul did in Ephesians 4:31 when he wrote, "Allow all bitterness, wrath, anger, quarreling, and slander to be taken out of you; and we can add all hatred to that list as well." Paul quotes Psalm 4:4 in Ephesians 4:26, in which he tells believers they ought to be angry. Of course, he includes the part of Psalm 4 that also reminds them they should not sin. It is like Paul acknowledges that all anger is not necessarily sin, but he knows how sinful people are and just ends up telling them it would be better to get rid of all of it. That understanding hinges on how you understand "all anger" though. It might mean "all anger" (i.e., every single bit of anger, regardless of circumstance and regardless of whether it leads one to think or act sinfully) or it might mean "all anger [without a justifiable reason]." It is also possible that a scribe looked at Jesus' words and thought it just sounded super harsh and impossible for everyone, so he went ahead and just added the word εἰκῇ (*eikē*). So which is more difficult to imagine—one of the aforementioned possibilities regarding the omission of the word or the idea that a scribe just thought Jesus sounded too harsh and decided to soften his command a little bit?

Regarding the actual content, we can ask ourselves, "Is Jesus' command more difficult with the word εἰκῇ (*eikē*) or without it?" Truth is you can argue this one either way as well. On the one hand, never getting angry is harder to do, but, on the other hand, equating all anger with sin, guilt, and judgment makes the reading without εἰκῇ (*eikē*) more difficult in light of other texts in the New Testament, such as when Jesus was angry in the temple or in Mark 3:5 where it says he looked at people "with anger." Remember what Jesus did in the temple, making a whip, driving out the vendors and moneychangers, and flipping over their tables (John 2:15). I am pretty sure Jesus smiled a lot during his ministry, but I promise you there was no smile while all that was going on.

Again, it is imperative that all of the evidence is considered. And we ought to point out that internal evidence is much more subjective than external evidence. This becomes pretty evident when we see the options for how someone can land their plane on the difficulty of a particular reading.

The Author's Style and Theology

Researchers must also consider an author's style and theology when thinking through a textual issue. For example, if there is a textual issue in the Gospel of Luke, we can compare a reading to the content found throughout the entire Gospel of Luke and we can also think through Luke's style in Acts. If Philippians, we want to weigh how Paul writes (e.g., his grammar, his choice of words, etc.) elsewhere in Philippians and the rest of his letters and we want to see how the theology in the respective variant readings compares to the overall theology of Paul in his other writings.

An issue in 1 Thessalonians presents an interesting opportunity to illustrate how text critics think through style. In 1 Thessalonians 2:7, some manuscripts read, "But we proved to be *gentle* (ἤπιοι *ēpioi*) among you, just like a nursing mother who tenderly cares for her own children." Other manuscripts read, "But we proved to be like *babies* (νήπιοι *nēpioi*) among you, just like a nursing mother who tenderly cares for her own children." The latter option seems to be more difficult because, if original, Paul would be using two different metaphors in very close proximity. It definitely looks a little confusing at first glance.

Some scholars point to Paul's style elsewhere as support for this reading. For example, in referring to himself, Paul might be switching from one metaphor in 1 Thessalonians 2:11 ("like a father") to another in 1 Thessalonians 2:17 ("made like orphans").[14] And we see another switch in Romans 8:19–22 and 23–25, the former referring to natural childbirth and the latter to adoption. These observations at least open up the possibility that Paul could have used two different metaphors in 1 Thessalonians 2:7. The examples in 1 Thessalonians 2:11, 17, and Romans 8:19–25, though, do not place two different metaphors in as close of a proximity as what we find in 1 Thessalonians 2:7. When someone compares style, they have to wrestle with examples like the ones provided here and decide for themselves whether or not they think the reading with "babies" fits Paul's style. And we should always remember that our literary sample is quite small when it comes to the authors of the New Testament. The sample of Paul's writings is obviously significantly larger than say Jude or James. But even what we have of Paul is limited. Therefore, we should be willing to at least think through the possibility that a reading does not conform to an author's style, which is why we consider the other external and internal evidences—all of it.

Parallel Passages

Parallel passages include places like the Synoptic Gospels, where there is a significant amount of similar material, letters like Ephesians and Colossians, in which Paul treats similar issues (e.g., Ephesians 6:1–9 and Colossians 3:20–25), and passages where a New Testament author quoted or alluded to a passage in the Old Testament. The consideration of parallel passages also includes certain apocryphal texts that are not found in the New Testament canon, since they sometimes contain similar material and date before the fifth century A.D.

---

14 Most translations leave out the "orphan" language when translating the verb in this passage. The NRSV is an example of one that includes it.

Take the beginning of Matthew 19:29 for example. Some manuscripts read, "And everyone who has left their homes, brothers, sisters, father, mother, children, or land . . ." And some manuscripts include "wife" in the series after "mother."[15] Compare that to Mark 10:29, which does not include "wife" but inverts the order of "father, mother," and then take a look at Luke 18:29, which has "house, wife, brothers, parents, or children." What happened here? Did a scribe try and harmonize what Matthew wrote with what Luke wrote? Or when a scribe was copying Matthew did they accidentally skip over "wife" like it appears at least one scribe did with "father"? Parallel passages are no doubt an important factor for certain textual issues.

PREFERENCE FOR CERTAIN TEXT-TYPES AND MANUSCRIPTS

For those that wrestle with issues of divergence among the host of New Testament manuscripts, it is absolutely imperative to nail down a method or at the least a set of guiding principles by which they can assess the evidence in favor of one reading over another. One group of manuscripts might read one way in a particular passage, while another group of manuscripts might read something different. It could be a word, could be a phrase, maybe a clause, maybe even a whole discourse unit. It is imperative that all of the evidence is considered though. Absolutely imperative. After all, whether a person just ignores the evidence or has a bias toward the evidence, the danger is all the same.

There is in the present day a wild consensus for preferentially adopting the reading of certain text-types and even certain manuscripts. I suppose it really started hard and fast just before turn of the twentieth century with Westcott and Hort's edition of the Greek New Testament (first published in 1881) and their unashamed proclivity towards two particular manuscripts (Codex Sinaiticus [known by the abbreviations ℵ or 01] and Codex Vaticanus [B or 03]), both of which belong to the Alexandrian text-type. I suppose before Westcott and Hort we could add the preference of many scholars for the Latin translation of the New

---

15 Some manuscript evidence leaves off "father," but this was most likely an accident.

Testament, even when there were Greek witnesses that challenged the reading of the Vulgate.

There is no such thing as a wholly trustworthy text-type. And, as A. T. Robertson pointed out, "[n]o single document, not even B, is always right."[16] Today, most researchers advocate for an eclectic methodology that incorporates all of the textual data. The problem is 01 and B still look like the favorites and researchers hardly deviate from them.[17] Are people really considering the evidence—all of the evidence, all of the possibilities? Or are textual critics and authors of New Testament commentaries just getting more skilled at masquerading their preference for 01 and B? Or maybe the people who write commentaries are not even really engaging the textual evidence like they should? This is just one of the reasons that more and more pastors and students of the New Testament in general should equip themselves with the skills they need to think through these issues for themselves.

---

16 A. T. Robertson, *Studies in the Text of the New Testament*, reprint ed. (Eugene, OR: Wipf and Stock, 2016), 91.
17 The only deviations really are when 01 and B do not agree and researchers find themselves in a conundrum of having to go against one or the other.

4

ENGAGING SOME MISCONCEPTIONS WITH TEXTUAL CRITICISM

There are several misconceptions associated with textual criticism. In the space that follows we are going to focus on three. The first deals with the hiddenness of the New Testament texts. Do we really know what they wrote? The second deals with the issue of inerrancy. And the third deals with why a certain change is needed in most local churches. Textual criticism is not to Christians what kryptonite is to Superman. The sooner that teachers in local churches start helping people understand how the New Testament was transmitted over the centuries, the better it will be for everyone. Of course, there are many more misconceptions worth considering,[18] but space is limited. I have been tasked with hitting a line drive, not a grand slam.

"We Have No Idea What They Wrote"

On occasion I have heard people say something like, "No one knows what the authors of the New Testament actually wrote." Is that actually the case though? Do we or do we not know what these authors wrote? There are a significant number of differences among

---

18 The one additional issue I wish I could treat here would have had the sub-heading "My Translation Is Better Than Yours." Permit me just one comment: I encourage all the students I teach to consult as many translations in as many languages of which they have a working knowledge. Besides the benefits of highlighting various lexical and syntactical issues that doing so affords students of the New Testament, in many cases it can help identify significant textual issues, as we saw in the introduction with Matt. 5:22. Anyone who champions a translation to the detriment of another, in my experience, does so out of selfish and foolish motives. There is no room for ESV-only, NASB-only, KJV-only, or any other only-this-particular-translation nonsense in the body of Christ. In fact, if we all were Bereans at heart, we would be "as-many-translations-as-I-can-get-my-hands-on" Christians and use them to help us mine God's Word for all the precious gems it contains.

the manuscripts of the New Testament. In fact, here Bart Ehrman is spot on: "No one knows for sure how many differences there are among our surviving witnesses, simply because no one has yet been able to count them all."[19] To this I might add, the world has yet to review all of the New Testament manuscripts, and that explains why no one has been able to count all the differences.

I recently went through just thirty manuscripts housed at the Vatican Library in Rome and marked all the differences between them and the first ever printed Greek New Testament[20] in the entire Gospel of Matthew.[21] In the 1,071 verses that make up the Gospel of Matthew, I located 1,698 places in which there was a difference in how the text reads, most of which are minor in nature with some more significant than others. That is pretty remarkable, for sure. Imagine what it would be for the rest of the New Testament. But such divergence does not mean that we do not know what the original authors of the New Testament texts actually wrote. Their texts are not lost. We can provide evidentiary arguments in favor of a particular reading where such divergence exists.

The presence of divergent readings among New Testament manuscripts is not a disqualifier for inspiration, just a reality. Divergent readings do not mean no one knows what the New Testament authors wrote, just that the study of the New Testament must ultimately begin with a textual analysis wherever such divergence is present. This raises the issue of preservation. Have the words—the original words penned by their authors—been preserved to the present day? Consider how Bart Ehrman describes the rationale for his coming to disbelieve in the divine inspiration of the Bible:

> This became a problem for my view of inspiration, for I came to realize that it would have been no more difficult for

---

19 Bart D. Ehrman, *Studies in the Textual Criticism of the New Testament* (Leiden: Brill, 2006), 309.
20 This edition of the New Testament was part of a Greek-Latin diglot, the fifth volume of the Complutensian Polyglot Bible. The New Testament was the first of six volumes, printed in Alcalá de Henares, Spain on January 10th, 1514.
21 Thomas W. Hudgins, "The Greek New Testament of the Complutensian Polyglot: Vatican Manuscripts and the Gospel of Matthew," PhD diss. (Universidad Complutense de Madrid, 2016).

God to preserve the words of scripture than it would have been for him to inspire them in the first place. If he wanted his people to have his words, surely he would have given them to them (and possibly even given them the words in a language they could understand rather than Greek and Hebrew). The fact that we don't have the words surely must show, I reasoned, that he did not preserve them for us. And if he didn't perform that miracle, there seemed to be no reason to think that he performed the earlier miracle of inspiring those words.[22]

"The fact that we don't have the words . . ." Pay special attention to those words. Actually this sort of reasoning is not uncommon in attempts to disprove biblical inspiration. Notice the argument really hinges on *not having the words*. The problem is we do have the words. At the least, humanly speaking—putting aside here the idea of providential preservation—we can be nearly certain that the original words of the New Testament have been preserved. Let me explain.

As I mentioned earlier, each time a manuscript was copied presented an opportunity for transcriptional mistakes and intentional changes. And it is reasonable to think this happened to some extent every single time one of these manuscripts was copied. Now if a manuscript was only copied once, this would raise an issue as far as preservation is concerned. But the original texts of the New Testament were not copied just once. For example, if Paul maintained a copy of his own letters so that they could be copied by Christian communities during his missionary travels, then he held on to the original and copies (plural) of the original were made throughout the Roman Empire. It is hardly unreasonable for someone to think each original would have been copied numerous times. And assuming they were, it is unlikely individuals who made copies of the originals would have made the exact same mistakes and intentional changes in transmission. Based on this, we can safely say we have the words, if we consider the manuscript evidence collectively.

The issue is not that we do not have the words. The problem is we have divergence among the extant manuscripts. Actually, we have more than what was originally written, considering some

22 Bart D. Ehrman, *Misquoting Jesus: The Story Behind Who Changed the Bible and Why* (New York: HarperCollins, 2005), 11.

scribes could have changed words or added phrases and clauses for a number of different reasons. Still, the issue is divergence. And divergence does not mean (1) that God did not do what Paul said he did in 2 Timothy 3:16 or (2) that the New Testament has not been preserved. Has it been immaculately preserved (i.e., every copy, every time, exactly like the original, without even the possibility of accidental or intentional changes to the text)? —No. But has it been preserved? —Clearly, and with great care in comparison to other literary works of historical significance prior to the invention of the printing press. Using the criteria outlined in chapter two, students of the New Testament are able to analyze these issues of divergence for themselves and make informed decisions about the original wording of the New Testament.

"The New Testament Is Not Really Inerrant"

The issue of inerrancy is directly tied to biblical inspiration. Sometimes people argue that the Bible is not inerrant if there really are all these textual issues in the New Testament, especially the more significant ones. The problem, though, is that inerrancy, just like inspiration, deals with the original composition of the biblical texts. The authority of the Bible hinges on our understanding of inerrancy.

There are issues where the worlds of inerrancy and textual criticism do not intersect. For example, people often point to the difference between Mark 6:8 and Matthew 10:9–10 and Luke 9:3. In the former, Jesus tells his disciples to take a staff, while in the latter two passages the disciples are told to not take one. There is an issue here, one which every Christian should be able to address. Now unfortunately is not the time. Our focus is on places where inerrancy and textual criticism do intersect. One of the most significant places is Matthew 1:7–8, where we find an issue with the reading Asaph (Ἀσάφ *Asaph*) versus Asa (Ἀσά *Asa*). The former is the name associated with a psalmist (1 Chronicles 25:1), the latter the name of one of Judah's kings (1 Kings 15:9ff.). Matthew is providing the genealogy of the heir to the Davidic throne, whose lineage traces back to Judah. Herein lies the issue: Asaph is a descendant of Levi, not Judah.

There are just a handful of solutions to this issue. One explanation offered by some is Matthew just plain got it wrong. The spelling could have been an accident originating from Matthew or, as Bruce Metzger suggested, Matthew could have reproduced the "erroneous spelling" (Asaph) he found in a genealogical list he consulted.[23] In other words, the origin of Asaph was not Matthew's fault per se, but his source's. In either, though, the problem is still there—an error would be present in Matthew 1:7–8.

Another explanation is that Asaph is just an alternate spelling of Asa.[24] Maybe this happened via transliteration, as Matthew carried the Hebrew into Greek, or perhaps certain people in the first century knew Asa as Asaph.

A final explanation is that Matthew intentionally changed the name or conflated two names to evoke theological parallels to another Old Testament figure and the life and ministry of Jesus (i.e., Asa refers to Asa [Ἀσά *Asa*], but Matthew added an extra letter [φ *ph*]) to connect Jesus to Asaph as well, though not saying Jesus was a physical descendant of Asaph). He could have been connecting Jesus' ministry to the prophetic role of Asaph, to how he sang God's praises, or to his priestly functions as a descendant of Levi. Vern S. Poythress, who opts for the latter, writes, "This allusion subtly suggests that Jesus is not only literally the heir to the kingly line of David, through king Asa, but figuratively and spiritually heir to the Levitical line of priestly activity."[25] Someone who agrees with this might explain the presence of Asa in some manuscripts by scribes not spotting Matthew's theological connection and thus smoothing out the text and removing any hint of historical confusion. Of course, this last explanation has its own hurdles to overcome, such as Jesus' priestly ministry is not likened to that of the Levites but rather to the priesthood of Melchizedek. Each explanation,

23 Bruce Manning Metzger, *A Textual Commentary on the Greek New Testament*, 2nd ed. (New York: United Bible Societies, 1994), 1.

24 James A. Borland mentions this as a possible explanation offered by Dan Wallace ("The Preservation of the New Testament Text: A Common-Sense Approach," *TMSJ* 10:1 [Spr 1999]: 49). This solution is provided in footnotes in the ESV and NLT.

25 Vern Sheridan Poythress, *Inerrancy and the Gospels: A God-Centered Approach to the Challenges of Harmonization* (Wheaton, IL: Crossway, 2012), 70.

though, has its own hurdles. But the hurdle facing option one is simply insurmountable. If Asa is not original, then there must be some other explanation than Matthew simply made a mistake in his composition or that he unwittingly reproduced an error found in a source consulted by him.

The problem in New Testament textual criticism stems from how inerrancy is misunderstood and how people, including evangelicals, overreach in their claims. Two chapters have appeared in recent years that directly address the issue of inerrancy and textual criticism: (1) John J. Brogan's "Can I Have Your Autograph?" and (2) Douglas Stuart's "Inerrancy and Textual Criticism."[26] Both are worth a careful read. Brogan points out three ways in which evangelicals have missed the mark with inerrancy and textual criticism: (1) some "ignore or minimize the extent of textual fluidity in the early church"; (2) some "misuse textual criticism to deny the validity of well-established and widely accepted text-critical methods"; and (3) some have tried to just explain away difficult passages by saying there must have been a manuscript somewhere someway that did not read the way we find it in all the rest.[27] We will come back to number one in subsequent section ("Christians Cannot Handle the Truth"). Evangelicals are not the only ones who have overreached at times though. Some who study the New Testament do so in hopes of finding an error on every single page—really in every single verse if it were possible. They do not start with an informed and logically founded conviction of divine inspiration, infallibility, and inerrancy. That totally changes how they view these textual issues and it also weakens the energy they are willing to expend in order to make sense out of a difficult reading.

There are difficult passages in the New Testament. There is no denying that. But there is no issue so difficult that the only educated option is to concede that the authors of the New Testa-

---

26 John J. Brogan, "Can I Have Your Autograph? Uses and Abuses of Textual Criticism in Formulating an Evangelical Doctrine of Scripture," in *Evangelicals and Scripture*, ed. Vincent Bacote et al. (Downers Grove, IL: InterVarsity, 2004), 93–111; Douglas Stuart, "Inerrancy and Textual Criticism," in *Inerrancy and Common Sense*, eds. Roger R. Nicole and J. Ramsey Michaels (Grand Rapids: Baker, 1980), 97–117.
27 Brogan, "Can I Have Your Autograph?," 102–106.

ment texts permitted—either knowingly so or otherwise—errors and untruths in their writing. And as daunting as is the number of textual issues and variants in the New Testament, it is not un-expected. Divergence in transmission in the pre-Gutenberg age was common. But divergence among extant manuscripts—which are copies—does not have any bearing on the inerrancy of the New Testament. Since God inspired the original author during the original act of composition, each of those texts was immediately inerrant upon completion.

Textual criticism matters because we do not get our transla-tions without first determining, via scientific analysis, the text of the New Testament. For most of the New Testament there is no serious question. Our modern translations of the New Testament, we can be sure, with differing philosophies of translation (e.g., some inten-tionally ambiguous and others more interpretive) bear the striking resemblance—the very likeness—of the original autographs. Where there are questions, the editors of those translations have attempted to bring the issue to the reader's attention via footnotes, brackets, etc., though to varying degrees.[28]

"Christians Cannot Handle the Truth"

I teach New Testament and Greek at an evangelical seminary. It surprises a lot of colleagues when I tell them that I begin teaching textual criticism in the seventh week of my Greek courses. Textual criticism is perhaps the hardest part of Greek exegesis for our stu-dents. Most students bring some knowledge about word studies and theology into a Greek course. Syntax is a different story because most students are lacking in even a basic knowledge of English grammar. The students that excel the most when it comes to syn-tax are generally those who have studied a language beyond their native tongue before taking a class on Greek. Syntax is difficult, but that is because syntax is basically everything when it comes to a language. Textual criticism is something else entirely and most students come into my classes with even less knowledge about it

---

28 See Appendix: "Textual Notes in Matthew 1–7."

than they do syntax—even though they most of them have spent years involved in a local church.

This book focuses on the church and helping individual believers understand why in the world we have notes at the bottom of some of the pages in our English Bibles regarding variant readings. The crazy thing is most Christians have never ever heard anything about manuscripts of the New Testament and divergent readings that exist among them. There is probably a plethora of reasons why, but the scariest reason to me is that leaders in local churches think that people's faith in biblical inspiration and inerrancy might be seriously hurt if they started talking about this stuff. Of course, the number one reason the topic never comes up in churches is probably because the equippers of those churches themselves have little to no knowledge about all this. Actually having studied something for oneself is a prerequisite to teaching others, or, as I tell my students, lack of real study translates into lack of real teaching.

Most Christians do not hear anything about textual criticism in their local churches. Does that seem a little strange to you? It does to me. And to be honest with you, if someone said it looks like Christians are not getting told the whole truth or that they are being shielded from some information, I might tend to agree . . . in part. If we just look around and observe the way this issue is treated in most Christian circles, it looks like the verdict is out: Christians apparently cannot handle the truth about the transmission of the New Testament texts. Of course, that is not true.

I recently asked my students the following question: "How can a pastor teach through the New Testament and something about helping the church understand the issue of inspiration and textual criticism never come up (not even in a Sunday School class)?" One student replied: "This topic can get confusing in a church setting. I think we would confuse them if we tell them about ancient Greek manuscripts and textual apparatuses." Another student wrote me:

> I have never heard anyone explain what was going on when different translations of the Bible added or subtracted words. We merely glossed over the discrepancy without an explanation. Unless someone expresses interest in these topics, I would not mention these subjects.

And here is one more reply:

> I can understand how pastors would tend not to bring up the textual issues in the local church. I am not saying this is the right avenue to take though. My thinking is that in some circumstances textual analysis could cause more harm than good in a congregation. Therefore, as a pastor, it is imperative that the under-shepherd know his flock. If he or she knows the flock, they will know how best to present the information and how much to present.

It might be easier to just skip over this whole issue of textual criticism, but easier is not better. I can imagine someone saying, "What they don't know won't hurt 'em." I disagree. It does not have to cause more harm than good. I think the people in our churches can handle some teaching on this matter.

I think the issue needs to be discussed more in our local churches so that no one gets the impression that it is being hidden from the faithful and, more importantly, so that every Christian will be strengthened (1) in their faith in Jesus and (2) their devotion to the Scriptures that make him known. Discussing textual criticism can anchor believers, so that they will not be tossed to and fro in their trust in the sufficiency and total veracity of God's Word, especially should they encounter someone who is super familiar with a book like *The Orthodox Corruption of Scripture* or *Misquoting Jesus* and the arguments found therein. Does everyone need to be a text-critical scholar? No. But should a knowledge about textual criticism be relegated to a select few? Absolutely not. We need more. We need better. And Christians should not be shielded from this information. Instead, churches need to do a better job of (1) studying the New Testament, (2) acknowledging that these textual issues exist, and (3) helping believers understand the transmission of the New Testament texts over the centuries, especially in the near millennia and a half before the invention of the printing press.

5

CONCLUSION

Textual criticism is extremely important for the study of the New Testament. No one who comes to the texts of the New Testament can do so without—at some point and in some way—engaging this area of exegesis. The original wording of the New Testament is not settled in every verse. That is why we find various notes at the bottom of our English translations. It is why we sometimes encounter bracketed verses, paragraphs even, in some translations. To study the New Testament is ultimately to study it all—even these textual issues. We have nothing to fear with textual criticism. In my opinion, it only bolsters the confidence we should have in our translations of the New Testament, that, to the extent that they faithfully communicate the original, author-intended message, they are inspired and inerrant, the very revelation of God to the world following the crucifixion, resurrection, and ascension of Jesus Christ. The words of the New Testament have been amazingly preserved in what is now approaching two millennia since that unrivaled demonstration of God's love on the cross at Golgotha. Though it has not been preserved immaculately, we have all we need at this point to reach reasoned and informed conclusions about the original wording of the New Testament where significant divergence is present. We ought to behold the New Testament in all its splendor. And textual criticism is a one of those necessary steps in exegesis if we hope to truly do so.

APPENDIX: TEXTUAL ISSUES NOTED IN MATTHEW 1–7

The table on page 33 demonstrates where textual notes are found in seven English translations for Matthew 1–7.[29] The translations included are: Holman Christian Standard Bible, New

---

29 E. Ray Clendenen and David K. Stabnow have gone through and noted the number of textual notes for Acts in twelve translations (See Chart 8.1 "Text-Critical Notes in Acts" in *HCSB: Navigating the Horizons in Bible Translations* [Nashville, TN: Holman, 2013]).

American Standard Bible, English Standard Version, New International Version, International Standard Version, New Living Translation, and the Revised Standard Version.

A few observations are worth noting here. The NASB and RSV do not mention manuscripts in their notes of Asa/Asaph and Amon/Amos in 1:7–8, 10. They only place a note with the alternate reading like "Gk *Asaph*." This is somewhat misleading since there is a question about the original text in these verses. The ambiguity in Matthew 1:7–8, 10 is difficult to understand, unless the editors were just trying to avoid pointing out a difficulty with the genealogy of Jesus. The ESV note for Matthew 1:18 reads, "Some mss *of the Christ*." Actually, there are four variant readings in this verse. Is it the birth of (1) Jesus, (2) Jesus Christ, (3) Christ Jesus, or (4) the Christ? The latter is the one that the ESV editors decided to highlight, even though options 2 and 3 are equally early.

It is quite striking to see how the HCSB includes significantly more textual notes than other translations, at least in Matthew 1–7. We need to be more forthcoming with these textual issues. Failure to do so gives credence to objectors and skeptics who argue that Christians pull the wool over the eyes of the faithful and shield them from data that they think could damage their faith. Of course, such data does is not inherently detrimental to a Christian's faith, but leaving notes out of our translations is far from being forthcoming with the readership publishers of modern translations hope to reach. The HCSB outshines other translations in this regard. The only one that compares is the ISV.

Textual divergence is a reality. Editors of future translations should consider textual notes where there is a significant question regarding the original reading of a passage in the New Testament. There is no reason why a note should not be placed in the text at Matthew 5:22, whether a person thinks "without a justifiable reason" is original or not. If so, there should be a note indicating that some manuscripts do not include the word; if not, then a note that some do.

	HCSB	NASB	ESV	NIV	ISV	NLT	RSV
1:6 "king"	x						
1:7–8 "Asaph"	x		x		x		
1:10 "Amos"	x				x		
1:18 "of the Christ"			x				
1:25 "her firstborn son"	x				x		
2:18 "lamentation and weeping"	x						
3:16 "for/to him"	x		x			x	x
4:10 "Get behind me"					x		
5:11 "falsely"					x		
5:22 "without a cause"	x		x	x	x	x	x
5:25 "judge will hand you over to"	x						
5:44 "bless those who curse you, do good to those who hate you,"	x					x	
5:44 "mistreat you and"	x						
5:47 "the tax collectors"	x				x		
6:1 "charitable giving"	x						
6:4 "openly"	x				x		
6:6 "openly"	x				x		
6:13 "For yours . . . . Amen."	x				x	x	x
6:15 "their wrongdoing"	x				x		
6:18 "openly"	x				x		
6:25 "or what you will drink"					x		
6:33 "of God"	x				x	x	
7:13 "For the way is wide and easy"			x				x
Total:	18	0	5	1	14	5	4

BIBLIOGRAPHY

Black, David Alan. "Jesus on Anger: The Text of Matthew 5:22a Revisited." *Novum Testamentum* 30 (1988): 1–8.

————— (ed.). *Perspectives on the Ending of Mark: 4 Views.* Nashville: B&H Academic, 2008.

—————, and Jacob N. Cerone (eds.). *The Pericope of the Adulteress in Contemporary Research.* Library of New Testament Studies. New York: Bloomsbury T&T Clark, 2016.

————— and Thomas W. Hudgins. "Jesus on Anger (Matt 5,22a): A History of Recent Scholarship." Pages 91–104 in *Greeks, Jews, and Christians: Historical, Religious, and Philological Studies in Honor of Jesús Peláez del Rosal.* Edited by L. Roig Lanzillotta and I. Muñoz Gallarte. Córdoba: El Almendro, 2013.

Borland, James A. "The Preservation of the New Testament Text: A Common-Sense Approach." *TMSJ* 10:1 (Spring 1999): 41–51.

Brogan, John J. "Can I Have Your Autograph? Uses and Abuses of Textual Criticism in Formulating an Evangelical Doctrine of Scripture." Pages 93–111 in *Evangelicals and Scripture.* Edited by Vincent Bacote *et al.* Downers Grove, IL: InterVarsity, 2004.

Clendenen, E. Ray and David K. Stabnow. *HCSB: Navigating the Horizons in Bible Translations.* Nashville, TN: Holman, 2013.

Ehrman, Bart D. *Misquoting Jesus: The Story Behind Who Changed the Bible and Why.* New York: HarperCollins, 2005.

—————. *Studies in the Textual Criticism of the New Testament.* Leiden: Brill, 2006.

Elliott, J. K. *New Testament Textual Criticism: The Application of Thoroughgoing Principles.* Supplement to *Novum Testamentum* 137. Edited by M. M. Mitchell and D. P. Moessner. Leiden: Brill, 2010.

Grisanti, Michael A. "Inspiration, Inerrancy, and the OT Canon: The Place of Textual Updating in an Inerrant View of Scripture." *JETS* 44:4 (December 2001): 577–598.

Hudgins, Thomas W. "The Greek New Testament of the Complutensian Polyglot: Vatican Manuscripts and the Gospel of Matthew." PhD diss. (Universidad Complutense de Madrid, 2016.

————. "The Ten Exegetical Steps" available at http://www.thomashudgins.com/p/resources.html

Metzger, Bruce Manning. *A Textual Commentary on the Greek New Testament.* 2nd ed. New York: United Bible Societies, 1994.

————. "Index of Versional Manuscripts of the New Testament." Pages 475–491 in *The Early Versions of the New Testament: Their Origin, Transmission and Limitations.* Oxford: Oxford University Press, 1977.

Poythress, Vern Sheridan. *Inerrancy and the Gospels: A God-Centered Approach to the Challenges of Harmonization.* Wheaton, IL: Crossway, 2012.

Robertson, A. T. *Studies in the Text of the New Testament.* Reprint ed. Eugene, OR: Wipf and Stock, 2016.

Robortello, Francesco. *De arte sive tatione corrigenda antiquorum libros disputatio.* Edited by G. Pompella. Naples: Luigi Loffredo Editore, 1975; cited by Tim William Machan, *Textual Criticism and Middle English Texts.* Charlottesville, VA: University Press of Virginia, 1994.

Stuart, Douglas. "Inerrancy and Textual Criticism," Pages 97–117 in *Inerrancy and Common Sense.* Edited by Roger R. Nicole and J. Ramsey Michaels. Grand Rapids: Baker, 1980.

Vaganay, León and Christian-B. Amphoux. *An Introduction to New Testament Textual Criticism.* Translated by Jenny Heimerdinger. New York: Cambridge University Press, 1991.

TOPICAL LINE DRIVES
Straight to the Point in under 44 Pages

All Topical Line Drives volumes are priced at $5.99 print and $2.99 in all eb-ook formats.

Available

The Authorship of Hebrews: The Case for Paul	David Alan Black
What Protestants Need to Know about Roman Catholics	Robert LaRochelle
What Roman Catholics Need to Know about Protestants	Robert LaRochelle
Forgiveness: Finding Freedom from Your Past	Harvey Brown, Jr.
Process Theology: Embracing Adventure with God	Bruce Epperly
Holistic Spirituality: Life Transforming Wisdom from the Letter of James	
	Bruce Epperly
To Date or Not to Date: What the Bible Says about Pre-Marital Relationships	
	D. Kevin Brown
The Eucharist: Encounters with Jesus at the Table	Robert D. Cornwall
The Authority of Scripture in a Postmodern Age: Some Help from Karl Barth	
	Robert D. Cornwall
Rendering unto Caesar	Chris Surber
The Caregiver's Beattitudes	Robert Martin
What is Wrong with Social Justice	Elgin Hushbeck, Jr.
I'm Right and You're Wrong	Steve Kindle
Words of Woe: Alternative Lectionary Texts	Robert D. Cornwall
Stewardship: God's Way of Recreating the World	Steve Kindle
Why Christians Should Care about Their Jewish Roots	Nancy Petrey
A Cup of Cold Water	Chris Surber
Pathways to Prayer	David Moffett-Moore
Jonah	Bruce G. Epperly
Ruth & Esther	Bruce G. Epperly
From Here to Eternity	Bruce G. Epperly

(The titles of planned volumes may change before release.)

Generous Quantity Discounts Available
Dealer Inquiries Welcome
Energion Publications — P.O. Box 841
Gonzalez, FL 32560
Website: http://energionpubs.com
Phone: (850) 525-3916

ALSO FROM ENERGION PUBLICATIONS

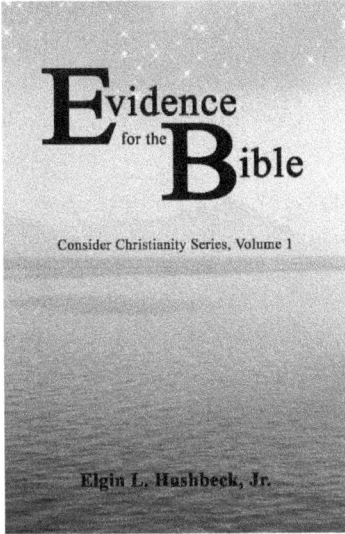

Hushbeck is truly a present day
champion in defense of Christianity and the Bible

Dr. Bob McKibben
Retired United Methodist Pastor
Atuhor of *The Gospel of Mark:
A Participatory Study Guide*

Evidence for the Bible
Consider Christianity Series, Volume 1
Elgin L. Hushbeck, Jr.

ALSO IN THE TOPICAL LINE DRIVES SERIES

Black uses his extensive knowledge
of the Greek language, the NT text,
and linguistics to amass a consider-
able amount of evidence to support
his case
Amazon.com Customer Review

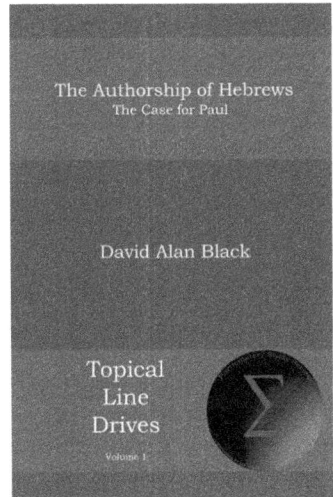

The Authorship of Hebrews
The Case for Paul

David Alan Black

Topical
Line
Drives

Volume 1

MORE FROM ENERGION PUBLICATIONS

Personal Study

Finding My Way in Christianity	Herold Weiss	$16.99
The Jesus Paradigm	David Alan Black	$17.99
When People Speak for God	Henry Neufeld	$17.99

Christian Living

Faith in the Public Square	Robert D. Cornwall	$16.99
Grief: Finding the Candle of Light	Jody Neufeld	$8.99
Crossing the Street	Robert LaRochelle	$16.99

Bible Study

Learning and Living Scripture	Lentz/Neufeld	$12.99
From Inspiration to Understanding	Edward W. H. Vick	$24.99
Luke: A Participatory Study Guide	Geoffrey Lentz	$8.99
Philippians: A Participatory Study Guide	Bruce Epperly	$9.99
Ephesians: A Participatory Study Guide	Robert D. Cornwall	$9.99
Evidence for the Bible	Elgin Hushbeck, Jr.	$16.99
When People Speak for God	Henry Neufeld	$17.99
Meditations on According to John	Herold Weiss	$14.99

Theology

Creation in Scripture	Herold Weiss	$12.99
Creation: the Christian Doctrine	Edward W. H. Vick	$12.99
Ultimate Allegiance	Robert D. Cornwall	$9.99
History and Christian Faith	Edward W. H. Vick	$9.99
The Journey to the Undiscovered Country	William Powell Tuck	$9.99
Philosophy for Believers	Edward W. H. Vick	$14.99

Ministry

Clergy Table Talk	Kent Ira Groff	$9.99
So Much Older Then ...	Robert LaRochelle	$9.99
Wind and Whirlwind	David Moffett-Moore	$9.99

Generous Quantity Discounts Available
Dealer Inquiries Welcome
Energion Publications — P.O. Box 841
Gonzalez, FL 32560
Website: http://energionpubs.com
Phone: (850) 525-3916

www.ingramcontent.com/pod-product-compliance
Lightning Source LLC
Chambersburg PA
CBHW021120020426
42331CB00004B/568